ANIMAL SAFARI

Lions

by Derek Zobel

BLASTOFF! READERS

BELLWETHER MEDIA · MINNEAPOLIS, MN

4/12

Note to Librarians, Teachers, and Parents:

Blastoff! Readers are carefully developed by literacy experts and combine standards-based content with developmentally appropriate text.

Level 1 provides the most support through repetition of high-frequency words, light text, predictable sentence patterns, and strong visual support.

Level 2 offers early readers a bit more challenge through varied simple sentences, increased text load, and less repetition of high-frequency words.

Level 3 advances early-fluent readers toward fluency through increased text and concept load, less reliance on visuals, longer sentences, and more literary language.

Level 4 builds reading stamina by providing more text per page, increased use of punctuation, greater variation in sentence patterns, and increasingly challenging vocabulary.

Level 5 encourages children to move from "learning to read" to "reading to learn" by providing even more text, varied writing styles, and less familiar topics.

Whichever book is right for your reader, Blastoff! Readers are the perfect books to build confidence and encourage a love of reading that will last a lifetime!

This edition first published in 2012 by Bellwether Media, Inc.

No part of this publication may be reproduced in whole or in part without written permission of the publisher. For information regarding permission, write to Bellwether Media, Inc., Attention: Permissions Department, 5357 Penn Avenue South, Minneapolis, MN 55419.

Library of Congress Cataloging-in-Publication Data

Zobel, Derek, 1983-
Lions / by Derek Zobel.
    p. cm. – (Blastoff! readers. Animal safari)
Includes bibliographical references and index.
Summary: "Developed by literacy experts for students in kindergarten through grade three, this book introduces lions to young readers through leveled text and related photos"–Provided by publisher.
ISBN 978-1-60014-608-4 (hardcover : alk. paper)
1. Lion–Juvenile literature. I. Title.
QL737.C23Z63 2011
599.757–dc22   2011005610

Printed in the United States of America, North Mankato, MN.

080111   1187

Contents

What Are Lions?	4
Prides	6
Hunting	14
Safety and Territory	18
Glossary	22
To Learn More	23
Index	24

What Are Lions?

Lions are strong, **wild** cats. Males are known for their thick **manes**.

Prides

Lions live in grasslands and forests. They form groups called **prides**.

Prides have males, females, and **cubs**. A pride can have between 3 and 40 lions.

Most lions in a
pride are female.
A pride can have
up to three
adult males.

male

female

Males and females in a pride have different jobs. Females care for cubs and hunt.

13

Hunting

Females **stalk** gazelles, zebras, and other animals. They like to surprise their **prey**!

The pride gathers around dead prey. Males usually eat first.

Safety and Territory

Males keep
the pride safe.
They chase away
animals that come
into their **territory**.

Males show their teeth to scare animals away. ROOOAAR!!!

Glossary

cubs—young lions

manes—thick hair on male lions; a mane covers the neck and head.

prey—animals that are hunted by other animals for food

prides—groups of lions; prides include males, females, and cubs.

stalk—to secretly follow

territory—the area in which an animal or group of animals lives

wild—living in nature

To Learn More

AT THE LIBRARY

Fatio, Louise. *The Happy Lion*. New York, N.Y.: Knopf Books, 2004.

Squire, Ann. *Lions*. New York, N.Y.: Children's Press, 2005.

Weeks, Sarah. *If I Were a Lion*. New York, N.Y.: Atheneum Books for Young Readers, 2004.

ON THE WEB

Learning more about lions is as easy as 1, 2, 3.

1. Go to www.factsurfer.com.

2. Enter "lions" into the search box.

3. Click the "Surf" button and you will see a list of related Web sites.

With factsurfer.com, finding more information is just a click away.

Index

adult, 10
cats, 4
chase, 18
cubs, 8, 12
eat, 16
females, 8, 10,
    11, 12, 14
forests, 6
gathers, 16
gazelles, 14
grasslands, 6
hunt, 12
jobs, 12
males, 4, 8, 10,
    11, 12, 16,
    18, 20
manes, 4
prey, 14, 16

prides, 6, 8,
    10, 12,
    16, 18
roar, 20
safe, 18
scare, 20
stalk, 14
strong, 4
surprise, 14
teeth, 20
territory, 18
wild, 4
zebras, 14

The images in this book are reproduced through the courtesy of: Eric Isselée, front cover; Ron Kimball / Kimballstock, p. 5; Theo Allofs / Masterfile, p. 7; Henry Wilson, pp. 7 (left), 21; Momentum, p. 7 (right); Peter Malsbury, p. 9; blickwinkel / Schmidbauer / Alamy, p. 11; Timothy Craig Lubcke, p. 13; Martin Harvey / Kimballstock, p. 15; Nabil Ezz / Photolibrary, p. 17; Joseph Van Os / Getty Images, p. 19.